COUNTRY
HOUSE

COUNTRY HOUSE

p

Janetta Hutchinson

This is a Parragon Publishing Book
This edition published in 2004

Parragon Publishing
Queen Street House
4 Queen Street
Bath BA1 1HE, UK

A copy of the CIP data for this book is available from the British
Library upon request.

ISBN 1-84273-531-4

Printed in China

CONTENTS

INTRODUCTION

Who at one time hasn't toyed with the idea of having a house in the country? With roses around the door, a thatched roof, the smell of baking coming from the kitchen, and perhaps a cat curled up in front of an open fire. It's the stuff of which dreams are made. Ask around, however, and you'll find that people's ideas on what makes a country house can differ greatly. At one extreme there's the elegant interior of a grand country mansion, all extravagant chintz drapes, polished wood, and fine furniture, and at the other the humble worker's cottage with its patchwork quilts and rag rugs.

Today's country house has distilled the decorating ideas from these two extremes, and what has evolved is the look we now call country style. Once ornate tapestries used to adorn the walls of the richest country mansions. Now tapestry fabrics or embroidered crewelwork fabrics can be found in a much more modest type of house. The beauty of country style, however, is that you don't need to have a house in the country to have a country-style home. Even if you live in the middle of a modern metropolis or in the suburbs, you can still easily achieve some of the delights of country style within your own home. In fact, today's country house may be found in a building never actually intended for human habitation—many people are renovating barns, farm outbuildings, cowsheds, and stables and turning them into lovely homes that boast as many original features as it was possible to maintain through restoration, as well as often superb country-style interior decorations.

What makes country style so special is that it's a look with roots in the past that is just as popular today. Country style is timeless. It's neither in nor out of fashion. The style is typified by informal wooden furniture, such as dressers, rocking chairs, and chests of drawers, and fabrics in a variety of patterns and colors from fancy florals to gingham and other checked designs. The trick to getting this particular interior design scheme right is to assemble it from items lovingly worn in, slightly frayed or faded, rather than those

that have obviously been bought brand new. This too is the joy of the country house. Where else would old, worn items be so cherished? In so many other interior design schemes the old has to make way for new contenders, but here a knock, chip, or blemish serves only to enhance. These imperfections add character and interest to pieces of furniture, and to the overall feel of the home, and are therefore admired. Better still, there's really no need to coordinate everything to the extreme; a careful mixture of patterns and colors positively enhances the overall effect. The result is an interior that gives the impression of having been lovingly put together over time, as though each piece had been handed down through the generations.

Interestingly, texture also plays a big part in interior decoration—stone, wicker, wool, lace, and brick are all found throughout the country house. They impart much of the necessary flavor that is key to achieving this style. With our current interest in all things organic, ecological, and natural, a second generation of materials is finding its way into the country house. Seagrass matting is becoming a popular choice—in appearance not dissimilar to the rush matting favored years ago.

Another element of this style is that of bringing the outdoors indoors, not just in relation to the materials in which things are made, but also with regard to pattern and color. Nothing says "country" more than a pretty floral design. Colors used indoors relate to those found outside. Sunshine yellow, sky blue, and grass green are all at home in the country house, be they painted on walls or used in fabrics. Earth tones such as beige, brown, and terra-cotta work just as well, particularly when teamed with an array of interesting textures.

Yet our love of the country house isn't just about the aesthetic appeal of the interiors of these homes. It's also about how such a home can evoke feelings of nostalgia for a time when life was seemingly simpler. In reality this wasn't necessarily the case—with no electricity, running water, or local stores, country life was often hard. Nevertheless, it remains true that country style makes us imagine a time when the sun always shone, birds sang, the flowers bloomed, and everyone was happy.

At the heart of a country home is the kitchen—a place that radiates warmth and to which the family gravitates. Indispensable to the country kitchen is a large dining table around which friends and family can gather. Add to this the smell of home cooking and you have the perfect ambience of the country home.

Today's country house has far more home comforts than those of yesteryear ever had. Many of the more modest homes were simply decorated with items chosen for their function rather than their aesthetic appeal. Originally, country homes were furnished with items made by traditional methods and decorated with traditional crafts such as patchwork. You'll find traditional style is still the key in today's country home, though it's likely that furniture and accessories will have been manufactured rather than handmade.

As the world gets smaller, the list of items that now fit the country style brief is getting larger, and foreign influences have been welcomed into the fold. Shaker style, originally created by a small religious sect who came to the United States from Britain more than two centuries ago, has enjoyed a huge revival both here and abroad, and the simple lines of this style fit in well with the aesthetic of a country kitchen. Elements once found in country homes on foreign shores are also making their way into American homes. Think of delftware, Chinese rugs, and Indian dhurries—a type of carpet. The result is that the country house has an ancestry that is both rich and poor, foreign and home grown, as decorative styles and furniture from diverse areas have amalgamated to create the country house we know and love.

*Bright, clean, busy or serene, the entrance sets
the scene for what lies in store inside the
country house. The entrance hall has a charm of
its own, both serving a practical purpose and
also acting as a showcase.*

ENTRANCES

above *This uncluttered entrance hall successfully combines several materials such as wood, stone, and natural-fiber flooring, which are all charmingly offset by a neat duck-egg blue and white color scheme.*

Welcome to the country house

You are on the threshold of discovering the secrets of the country house. Whether you are looking for the style of a cozy country cottage, a farmhouse or a grand manor house, the importance of the look and feel of the entrance hall cannot be overestimated. It is the key to the whole atmosphere of the home.

Years ago, cottages did not boast the luxury of an entrance hall, as the front door opened into one single room which was the living area. It was only later that cottages with two rooms downstairs and two upstairs were built, but these again would almost certainly never have had an entrance hall. Usually the doors to these homes would open directly into either the kitchen at the back of the house, or the living area at the front. On the other hand, a country manor house would feature an entrance hall possibly the size of several ordinary rooms, and in the grandest of homes it would have included a fireplace, furniture, and enough art hanging on the walls to rival a gallery.

Essentially the entrance hall in today's country house serves a dual purpose. On a practical note, the hall is the gateway from the outside world into the interior of the home, which means it has a lot to cope with. An endless trail of wet feet, muddy paws, and dripping umbrellas can cause wear and tear on a daily basis. Occasionally the entrance hall is the place where shopping, heavy loads, and deliveries are received. With all this activity going on, it most certainly stands to reason that the decorations used here must be robust enough to withstand the elements, yet be easy enough to clean when they suffer from their effects.

Terracotta, dusky and pale pink color schemes work very well in the country house. A touch of spring green provides a complementary but interesting color combination.

left *Teaming reclaimed wooden floorboards with stone flooring makes for an attractive and very practical entrance hall.*

right *A country scene painted in oils in the triangular panel on the interior of the front door makes an amusing little detail and indicates things to come.*

Flooring choices

Entrance hall flooring must be tough. Traditionally, stone or tiles were used in the entrances to most homes. Patterned encaustic tiles, whose design was formed by inlaying different colored clays which fused together when fired, or marble, the most expensive of all stone floors, was preferred in the larger, richer houses. Properties of more modest means would use simple unglazed quarry tiles or flags cut from local stone. Interestingly, what was once considered the poor man's choice is now valued as a very desirable option; the cost of simple quarry tiles, terra-cotta, or stone flooring can actually be quite high because we are no longer limited to using stone sourced from local quarries. Today it is perfectly common for a country house to boast stone flooring that has traveled from as far afield as France or Spain. So what is historically the cheaper option can actually work out to be quite expensive. Nevertheless, stone does provide a very attractive, strong, and easy-to-clean floor that will last for many years, which is just the type of floor an entrance hall demands.

Wood flooring runs a close second in the range of floor coverings suitable for the entrance to a country house, as this material is also fairly easy to maintain. In the earliest country houses the wooden floors were

left *This impressive staircase has simply been painted white, and to keep noise levels down it has been partially covered with a cream carpet.*

below and opposite *Nothing says "country" better than terra-cotta floors, and this well-worn example is quite a feature of this entry. The faded floral draperies and the vintage child's toy all add to its appeal.*

above With a little lobby by the front door to take care of coats and shoes, the main entrance doubles as a living area. The old pine settle piled with pillows is very inviting and there's room for a table and chair too.

left and right Pine furniture makes a country home. Painted furniture looks particularly good when it's distressed—the scratches and chips all add to its appeal.

hand-cut planks which were fairly wide and of random width. They were generally left unfinished, though softwoods were sometimes painted in a solid color or to resemble hardwoods. Any wood floor, from reclaimed floorboards to solid hardwood, has a place in the country house, for two main reasons: first, because wood has traditionally been used indoors as flooring; and second, because wood is natural and so fits the brief for a country-style interior design scheme. The trend today is for country interiors to incorporate "natural" elements, whose textures and obvious links to the outdoors and countryside enhance the country feel.

Blue and yellow always make for a vibrant color scheme. Its use is especially suited to country houses as it will bring a fresh, outdoors feel to any room. Checked fabrics in natural fibers such as cotton or linen are well suited to this look.

Some country houses also boast attractive brick floors. The use of brick may start on the porch, if there is one, progressing through to the entrance hall and possibly into the kitchen. This is an example of how flooring choices have come full circle—several hundred years ago brick was one of the cheapest forms of flooring, often used in simple country cottages as well as in the basements and cellars of larger houses. Today it has again found favor in the country house, this time because it can be used to create an interestingly textured floor. In some country homes rugs are placed on the entrance hall floor. Years ago they were used as a form of insulation, to take the chill off a cold stone floor—but in country-style homes today a rug on the floor is usually placed there more for decorative effect than for the practical purpose of protecting the floor from dirt and excessive wear.

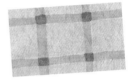

Color schemes and decoration

The second function of the entry is to serve a decorative purpose. As soon as you step inside the entrance hall your first impression of the house is formed. So it stands to reason that the decorations you choose to use here are vitally important. Our interest in interior design today means no aspect of the home is overlooked, as the chance to create, display, and visually improve will result in no area being left untouched. Years ago only in the entrance halls of grander homes would interior decoration have been given such consideration. Certainly, if any more modest country house was lucky enough to have an entrance hall, it was there merely to serve a practical purpose. But these days the entry is used to set the scene, offering a visual taster of things to come.

There are no hard and fast rules about color schemes for the entrance hall of a country house. Any shade from white or pale pastels through to bright colors can be used. The choice depends on what type of impression you wish to create. The entrances in the homes shown here all gain something different from the colors in which they have been painted.

Pastel shades are easier on the eye, and are a particularly good choice when you wish to add interest to an area subtly. In some of these entrance halls the clever use of pastels on the walls serves to enhance the hall's other features. For example, the powder blue walls on page 13 pick up the muted blue tones in the flooring, and the soft pink walls on pages 16–17 resonate with the pinky hues found in the terra-cotta floor.

Taking color to the other extreme, bright shades always have impact. Yellow gives the hall on page 18 a sunny disposition, and is a good color choice when natural light is limited, as is often the case in entrance halls, which may have only small windows or perhaps none at all. The use of red is very dramatic. You definitely wouldn't have found this color in many cottages in former times; however, because today's country house doesn't slavishly re-create former styles but simply takes inspiration from the past, a certain amount of artistic license is allowed. In the house shown opposite, one of the reasons red works so well is that it echoes the richness and depth of color of the entry's other decorations. Normally, decorations of this quality would have been found in grander country houses, and it is in these same homes that red may have been used to decorate the walls. Acknowledged as a good background for pictures, it was a popular shade in the early 1800s; and in Victorian times, with the development of chemical dyes, decorating in bright colors was all the rage. This entrance hall is by no means situated in such a grand house, but cleverly its interior decoration pays them homage.

The entrance hall is also a place for storage—coats, boots, and umbrellas all need a home here. While in the past simple pegs on

opposite Rough plastered walls painted a vibrant shade of red are a fantastic choice for this small entrance hall. The color is echoed in the rugs, bar stool (below), and floral design of the umbrella stand. A white ceiling prevents the color scheme from appearing too oppressive.

below The use of rugs not only visually breaks up the expanse of floorboards, but protects them too.

the wall or the back of the door would have sufficed, in today's country house storage has been taken to a new level. The way in which such items are kept has become a point of interest in itself. A stand or container filled with umbrellas and walking sticks both serves a purpose and makes an attractive feature, as does a line of boots by the door. In other houses such basic items as these may be hidden away in a closet or in a cupboard beneath the stairs, but as these things are intrinsic to country life their presence actually goes some way to creating country style.

Furniture and accessories

Furniture can also be used in the entrance hall. Its presence is dictated more by the space available than by whether or not its positioning is true to original country homes. Some form of seating is particularly desirable here—it is always preferable to sit on a chair rather than the stairs when pulling boots on and off. Certainly a little table, shelf, or cupboard is handy to take care of the clutter that accumulates. As long as you pick furniture designed in traditional style, there's no doubt it'll blend in perfectly. At the other extreme a very large entrance hall can almost become a family room in its own right. If there's space for a sofa or dining table the hall can double as an informal living space or dining area.

As some of the entrance halls shown here demonstrate, a pine settle is made quite comfortable with the addition of a seat pad and plenty of pillows; and a large, squashy sofa similarly piled high with pillows makes an inviting addition to a rather grand entrance. The idea of creating a living room in the actual entrance hall again harks back to the days when the door to most cottages really did open straight into the living area. Today, if you are lucky enough to have an entry of a substantial size then it's a great opportunity to decorate your home in two distinct styles. A fairly informal decorating scheme will tend to work well in such a large entrance hall, and this leaves the actual living room or dining room available for decoration in a more formal manner.

As for which accessories to use in this area of the house, almost anything goes. From pictures, paintings, books, and barometers to some more unusual

left *Simple white walls provide a neutral background on which to display a variety of pictures. Wall-to-wall natural flooring adds texture, and the umbrellas make a colorful feature.*

contenders such as rocking horses, clocks, and chandeliers, anything that invokes a country feel can have a happy home here. As long as the pictures, be they etchings, sketches, watercolors, or oils, bear a country-related theme, then they will be suitable for the walls of the country house. And what better place to put a barometer than in the entrance hall? This item, both functional and decorative (it is used for predicting the weather), is ideal for placing by the door so you can give it a quick check before heading out. Like the grandfather clock, this is an item that would have been found only in grander country houses but is now very much at home in more modest surroundings. Children's toys, such as the wooden horse on page 17, would certainly have been banished to the nursery in days gone by, but now can make an amusing piece to display in the entrance hall. And this, in essence, is what today's entrance halls are all about—an acknowledgement of styles from the past and a chance to have some fun while creating your country home.

left *A silver hanging candelabra, bearing real candles and covered in ivy, offers a very decorative form of lighting for this unique entrance hall.*

opposite *This wonderful entrance hall is quite easily achieved. The walls are roughly plastered, and the stunning spiral staircase makes a great focal point. The damask sofa covered with a rich-colored throw and some tasselled tapestry pillows is very inviting, while a large wicker basket takes care of discarded reading matter.*

As the heart of the country home, the kitchen is so much more than just a place to cook. Warm, welcoming, and full of interest, it's easy to while away the hours cocooned in its splendor.

KITCHENS

A timeless look

There's no denying the irresistible appeal of a country-style kitchen. Even the most tidy-minded among us can't resist rummaging through the variety of china displayed on a Welsh dresser, or gazing in wonder at an intriguing assortment of pots, pans, pitchers, and utensils hanging from a beamed ceiling. In fact, this Aladdin's cave of decorations is now synonymous with the country kitchen.

It is almost a prerequisite to have virtually everything you own on show in order to create a typical country kitchen. There's a homey, old-fashioned feel to these busy kitchens, which ties in very well with the nostalgic appeal of country homes. With utensils, pots, and pans on show the kitchen looks ready for action—as though someone may be about to brew some coffee or take a freshly baked cake out of the oven. In former times the kitchen was very much a working room and a hive of activity. Items most used were kept in easy reach of the cook, although there would have been far fewer items actually in use than you will find decorating a country kitchen today. In many cottages the kitchen also doubled as the living room, and was perhaps the only downstairs room in the house.

Every item had to earn its keep, and every inch of space in these tiny houses had to be utilized. The ceiling was also made use of for hanging dried flowers and bunches of herbs. Today this is usually just for decoration, but in former times these items would have been brought indoors and hung to dry in the warmth of the kitchen. Baskets of vegetables and bowls of fruit are all part of the picture and along with bunches of flowers are much in evidence in the country kitchen. The presence of these natural elements adds color and texture, creating a "living" display. The impression they create is very earthy and organic, as though the owner of the home had just picked them fresh from the garden, or perhaps just

right Originally the range wasn't just used for cooking—it provided heat too and was often used for drying clothes. With a cat curled up on the chair and clothes hung up to dry, this scene is typical of country kitchens, especially those from years ago.

returned from the vegetable market. Again, this contributes to the idea that the country kitchen is the hub of the home, a place for working and also enjoying life, where all manner of activities take place.

To the untrained eye it may seem at first that the country kitchen is in disarray. However, its owner will know exactly where everything is kept. Pots and pans are usually hung near the stove, storage jars and spices stand on the countertop or windowsill, dishes and plates are kept permanently in the draining rack, glassware is shown off safely on the shelves, and larger heavier items, such as mixing bowls and serving dishes, are stored below the counter.

The joy of creating a country kitchen is often in the purchase of these items. Who can deny the pleasure of hours spent rifling through antiques shops and secondhand shops in pursuit of items to display in the kitchen? A single visit to a department store won't achieve the same result, because the key to creating an interesting country kitchen is to collect these accessories over time, and enjoy the search. From pots and pans to ceramics, glassware and utensils, baskets and storage jars, the majority of kitchen implements on show are items that should be chosen not just for their practical worth but also for their looks.

opposite *This kitchen's color scheme is really appealing. The yellow walls offset the blue and white china and fabrics perfectly, and a burst of color from the flowers adds impact.*

right *The kitchen is the heart of the country home, and a wood stove or an old-fashioned range such as an Aga is essential for imparting true country flavor to the room.*

Storage and display

A dresser (or hutch), plate rack, or other form of shelving packed full of ceramics is the cornerstone of the country kitchen. The dresser, as we know it today, with its tall upper section of display shelves, appeared in the 1700s. Until then wooden platters or polished pewter plates were the norm, but as ceramics became cheaper to buy, dinner services were displayed on the dresser. Depending on the fashion for household decoration, dressers have moved from entry hall to dining room to parlor to kitchen, but by the late 1800s they had taken up residence primarily in the kitchen, and large 18th-century farmhouses were known for their elm and oak dressers. Later, pine became the wood most commonly used for them. The shelves of the dresser are called the rack, and this is positioned over a wider base, which can vary in design. The term Welsh dresser is now sometimes used to describe any dresser with cupboards in the base. A dresser with an open area in the base between the cupboard doors is known as a "dog kennel" dresser; it was in this open area that the soup tureen from the dinner service was displayed.

A perennial favourite in American kitchens is the wooden pie safe. Though the pierced patterns in the tin doors are decorative, their original purpose was to let in air while keeping out flies. Today, if you wish to show off an attractive display on the shelves inside, simply leave the doors wide open. A jelly cabinet, with its wire door inserts, can be used in a similar way. Wall-hung wooden plate racks or simple wooden shelves edged with lace trim are other methods of displaying decorative items in the kitchen.

The palette of blues, creams, and yellows suits the feel of the country house superbly. The blues echo the delftware and pottery, and the butterscotch shades are seen in the enamel of Agas and other country-style kitchen ranges.

left *Fresh produce is synonymous with the country house. A bowl full of fruit on display is a must.*

right *A modern metal pendant light has been given a country-style touch simply by being trimmed with a piece of lace.*

above *This lovely room boasts all that a country kitchen should have: pretty china, tureens, jugs and jars, fresh fruit and flowers, lace trimmings, and pine furniture. The old stone walls are painted white which provides a perfect background for the displays.*

This is not the place to practice minimalism. The more you can pack onto your kitchen shelves, the more attractive your kitchen will seem. Mix and match is the name of the game, but in some cases a loosely coordinated collection of china can also look good. Those who find the heady mix of color, pattern, and shape too much may decide to impose some semblance of order and limit the range of china on show to one particular dinner service, simple earthenware, or specific color scheme—the striking blue and white designs of delftware or Willow Pattern pottery, for example. Whether you decide to introduce some aspect of coordination into this array of ceramics is up to you. Another way to make the most of kitchen shelving is to use it to show off collections. Anything from teapots to milk jugs or coffee mugs has a place here—and if you happen to collect more than one type of item, you could always display one collection per shelf.

Today's country kitchen is at best a visual acknowledgment of its former self. Our homes and standards of living have progressed so much that although re-creating a realistic country kitchen isn't impossible, many of us would find it hard to do without the modern appliances we're accustomed to. The most we can hope for is to take elements from the rooms of the past and incorporate them into 21st-century living. Interestingly, designers of the most progressive kitchens today are actually harking back to the styles of yesteryear, and the fashion for freestanding cabinets is emerging once again, after years of built-in, streamlined kitchens ruling the roost. But there is one big difference: dishwashers, washing machines, fridges, and freezers are now all very much part of kitchen design. It's essential to keep as many of these modern appliances out of sight as possible—hidden away behind cupboard doors, or simply curtained off beneath a countertop—if you want to replicate the true feel of a country kitchen.

The Aga

There's one item you won't find hiding behind closed doors and that's the range. Nothing epitomizes the country kitchen more

opposite The salmon pink walls of this delightful kitchen help create a cozy atmosphere, and with the table set for a meal the room looks very inviting.

above The hotplates of the Aga are ever ready for use and the rail provides a place to hang and dry dish towels and oven gloves. Copperware is also very much at home in the country kitchen.

below Floral fabrics are a must in the country house. The delicate pattern of this material is a suitable choice, because any larger designs would be lost in the folds of the cloud shade.

below *The vibrant yellow walls and tablecloth give this dining area a sunny disposition. The use of blue in the paneling below the window and in the chairs and picture frames balances the color scheme, offering contrast without becoming overpowering.*

than an old-fashioned wood stove or kitchen range. Originally cooking was done over open fires in the hearth, then when the use of the wood stove and the coal stove became more common during the 19th century, these were positioned in the hearth. Wood and coal stoves were eventually supplanted by the kitchen range, but in the second half of the 20th century the wood stove once more became a feature of the country home.

Also highly appropriate for a country kitchen is an old-fashioned style of range, such as the Aga, which has recently begun to be imported from Britain. Originally developed in the 1930s and fired by solid fuel, the Aga is now powered by electricity, gas, or oil. It can perform a multitude of tasks, including providing up to four radiant-heat ovens of different temperatures, and hotplates that vary in temperature. Because it is always on, it also warms up the kitchen and provides hot water. The heat a range such as this gives off is welcome on winter days, and in the past a clotheshorse with laundry to dry would be placed in front of it, or an airer suspended from the ceiling could be dropped down to dry clothes. Black-leaded ranges have long been superseded by ceramic, offering color options such as green, yellow, red, or blue.

Temper light bright colors such as yellow with deeper contrasting hues such as blue for a successful color scheme. Fabrics with heavy weaves and slubs, and of course florals all add interest.

Materials and furniture

Wood and tiles are the two main surface materials of choice in a country kitchen. For the floor and work surfaces, the choice is interchangeable. Both have certain pros and cons. Wood is more comfortable underfoot, warmer, and less harsh than tiles—drop something on this floor and there's a chance it may not break. Tiles

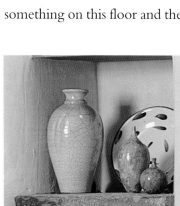

left When displaying china, be it on a small shelf or on a dresser, prop platters and plates at the back, and put vases, mugs, jugs, and bowls in the foreground. Groups united by color always work well.

right Simple muslin curtains with tie-tops make a lovely window treatment. Here they are hung on a narrow wooden curtain pole which complements the old wooden beam above the window.

are harder, colder and, in the case of countertops, a little less easy to keep clean, as dirt can quickly collect in the grout. Because of their propensity for coolness, though, tiles are a good choice, especially if you prepare a lot of pastry or handle meats. Interestingly, tile-topped tables are making an appearance in the kitchen too, as an alternative to that mainstay of the country kitchen, the traditional pine table.

Pine furniture is an essential feature of the country house, in particular the country kitchen. As a cheaper alternative to other woods, pine was originally used when money was tight, but now pine furniture is a staple in the country home. In the kitchen the pine dresser, pine dining table, and pine chairs are all part of the country brief. Of course, you can deviate from pine and still create a country kitchen. All woods look good. But this isn't the place for highly polished pieces—the more rough and rustic the better. Pine that has mellowed with age is more suitable than modern pine, with its yellowy newness, so choose secondhand items if you can for that appealing worn-in appearance. If you haven't space for a pine dresser, then a wooden cupboard used to form a base, with several shelves positioned above it on which to display your china, works just as well. Metal hinges and ceramic or wooden knobs on doors and drawers also add to the country flavor—and increasingly wrought iron is being brought into the fold.

The dining table is the centerpiece of the country kitchen. Before the advent of work surfaces, nearly all the kitchen's activities took place on the table—cooking, cleaning, polishing, dining, and even sleeping, as an unexpected guest was given the table for a bed. In former times carpenters assembled the tables in situ; nowadays you may have trouble getting a large table through the door, if indeed there is floor space for it in your kitchen. Space permitting, the kitchen table should be large enough to allow all the family to dine together. Round tables are great as they can easily accommodate extra guests when the chairs are squeezed together. The size of today's kitchen may limit your choice of table, and a gateleg table is a good investment when space is tight. You have more scope with what type of dining chair to choose. Windsor chairs with their

left *An old-fashioned apron sink positioned on bricks creates space so a cupboard can be built in underneath. Brass faucets in a traditional style complete the look. The edges of the countertop overlap the sink slightly for drainage without drips.*

opposite *Boasting beautiful beams, a terra-cotta floor, pine furniture, and a range, this country kitchen contains all the essential elements. The tiles on the wall and in the hearth feature country animals.*

traditional saddle-shaped seats, high or low curved bow backs, and U-shaped arms are firm favorites in the country kitchen, since they were designed in the early 18th century. Simpler spindle or ladderback chairs are just as welcome. Even a long pine bench or settle makes a suitable choice for kitchen seating. These pieces were popular centuries ago, when the settle would have been positioned by the fire, its high back used to stop drafts. The seat can be left bare or made more comfortable with the addition of a seat pad. Rush-seated chairs are also an excellent choice, their presence bringing a more Mediterranean country flavor into the kitchen.

The white porcelain apron sink, which dates back to Victorian times, has been adopted as the sink of choice in many a country home. When it was originally made it would have been found more often in the kitchens of grand Victorian houses than in a cottage kitchen, which may well have had a rough stone sink. However, the apron sink is now considered so appropriate for the country home that several kitchen-cabinet manufacturers have included modern versions in their ranges in order to satisfy demand. No longer is it necessary to search high and low for one in architectural salvage yards.

Faucets would have been unheard of in a true country kitchen. Running water wasn't an option in most homes and when supplies did improve in the mid to late 1800s it was mainly the grand houses not the country cottages on the receiving end. Today, of course, all homes have a water supply, so when creating a country kitchen any Victorian style of faucet is fine, be it wall- or sink-mounted, or a faucet with an arched swan's neck design.

Green and cream always make a great team. Combine stronger peppermint greens with buttermilk colors, or put softer, lighter pastel shades alongside gentler vanilla creams.

left *The manner in which a couple of glasses almost overflowing with flowers and a basket full of garden produce are displayed on the table demonstrates the casual approach one should have toward country style.*

right *Painting the door frame green highlights this door's attractive shape, and the metal hardware increases its appeal.*

below *This kitchen is designed around a simple color scheme of green and cream. The furniture is minimal—just a table, chairs, and cupboard—but the impact is huge, thanks to the abundance of flowers and vegetables. It's easy to see this is a busy working kitchen.*

Look upward in the country house and you'll most likely see wooden beams. Centuries ago most homes were constructed so that the beams and joists of the floor above were left exposed, and perhaps only the undersides of the floorboards were given a plaster covering. Although the fashion for suspended plaster ceilings, which hid the beams and were often ornately decorated, prevailed in richer homes, in country cottages lack of money meant that beams remained very much part of the interior. Decorating them became par for the course. Dried flowers, hops, bunches of herbs, and baskets can all be found dangling from the beamed ceilings of country houses, with the space in between the beams painted white or sometimes colored for a more decorative effect.

Color schemes

There is no particular color in which to paint a country kitchen. With so many accessories, furnishings, and furniture providing an assortment of colors, there's no real requirement to paint the room anything other than white. The kitchen will never look dull because so much else adds interest to the room. However, the use of color can offset decorations or unite several colors, giving coherence when too many hues can cause disorder. Yellow is an excellent choice for the walls, for several reasons. It certainly cheers up the room, and if not much natural light is available, the brightness of this shade will help create the illusion of light. If you are going for such a bright color in your kitchen, a simple flat coat of paint is not the only option. Paint techniques such as sponging or colorwashing result in a more mottled effect so the intensity of the color is reduced. The unusual use of red in the room shown opposite works well as a subtle contrast to the brown shades found in the brick, wicker, and wood. Oriental rugs placed on the floor echo the red in the ceiling and cleverly provide balance.

When choosing paints look carefully at what's on offer from paint companies. Some have a palette of "historical shades" based on those used in houses centuries ago, and this can make all the difference in creating an authentic atmosphere.

opposite The red walls and ceiling and blue-gray beams and door make for a very exciting, though quite unusual, color scheme. The browns of the terra-cotta floor, furniture, baskets, and brickwork provide contrast and balance to the scheme.

below Grandfather clocks wouldn't have been commonplace in most country cottages. But today their presence has nostalgic appeal while their decorations can fit in nicely with country color schemes.

Coziness is the key to an authentic country living room. A sumptuous sofa piled high with pillows and throws, placed near a roaring fire, will help your home boast true country style.

LIVING ROOMS

The fireplace as focus

Warm, cozy, and comfortable—the living room is a place to relax, a retreat from daily pressures, and a place where the family really feels at home. The fireplace is absolutely key to this atmosphere.

Today's country-house living rooms can range in style, emulating the grandeur of Federal or Victorian parlors with fine furniture, marble fireplaces, and impressive window treatments, or harking back to humble cottage-style dwellings, sparse in furniture and furnishings. Nowadays most country homes use a cross-section of these styles, put together and adapted to suit the taste and requirements of the home owner and the architecture of the house.

The focal point of the living room in a country house is the fireplace. Its original purpose in the home was to provide warmth and light on dark nights, and in the most humble one-room abodes it was the place to cook and heat water too. These days, however, its presence in a country house is more for aesthetic reasons than practical purposes. Today's homes rarely suffer from the cold, and the use of the fireplace, once the most important functional item in the room, has changed. A real fire first and foremost offers decorative interest, a focal point, and a chance to re-create the look of homes from years ago. That said, nothing beats a real fire, and nothing evokes a true country image more than a dog curled up on a rug in front of the fire, or a family relaxing around the fire on a cold winter's evening. There may be only a few occasions when you put it to use, on particularly cold winter days, but the joy of seeing real flames dancing in the grate justifies having a working fire in the room.

left This beautiful fireplace is obviously the focal point of the room, and it is further enhanced by the balanced layout of the furniture. The glass coffee table offers respite in an otherwise richly colored room.

The type of fireplace can vary from a large inglenook, popular in previous centuries when built-in seating within the inglenook was a common feature, to a splendid marble fireplace, which gives the room an upscale air, or a simple little fireplace with a pine mantelpiece. In years gone by, each of these styles would have had a place in a particular style of home. The more important the room, the bigger the fireplace. The material from which the mantelpiece was made also followed a hierarchy. White marble was the first choice for main rooms, but by the 1900s wooden mantels rivaled their popularity in expensive homes.

Today some cross-pollination has occurred, and styles of fireplaces that aren't strictly true to country properties are being found within these homes. Yet the fact remains that a real fire is the very essence of a country-style living room and it is more important to have than not to have in this case. The more recent gas "coal effect" fires will never be the real thing, but many models are very convincing, with the fake coals glowing just like real coals, and because they don't produce ash they require a lot less work.

The classic color combination of red, green, and cream has stood the test of time in the country house. These creamy yellow walls are enhanced by a variety of fabrics, be they florals or stripes, all featuring russet red and bottle green shades.

below and left *Sometimes pets can provide inspiration for your choice of finishing touches. Here china dogs and a tapestry cushion offer a cute little "mini-theme'" to the main design scheme.*

above *This living room combines two distinct styles—the grand fireplace, with brass fender and ornately decorated mantelpiece, is very manor house, but the table covered with a floor-length cloth and home to an array of photographs is far more country cottage.*

below *The presence of so much pine paneling painted white gives this room a nautical feel that is further enhanced by the display of ships and seabirds on the end wall. Wood and wicker add contrast to an otherwise pale color scheme.*

When your fire is not in use, or if you prefer not to use it at all, then it can double as a wonderful display area. Vases of dried flowers or even fresh flowers are often placed in unused fireplaces, to good effect. Other accessories are perfectly at home here. Firescreens, originally used to diffuse the heat from the fire when ladies were sitting nearby, provide an attractive way to cover an empty grate. Alternative ideas include piling pinecones up in the grate, or displaying a collection of tall pillar candles on the hearth.

Furniture and fabrics

Because the fireplace was the main attraction in the living room, furniture was naturally arranged around it. A sofa in front of the fire, with maybe an armchair or two either side of the fire, is a typical arrangement. Then, space permitting, other furniture such as a footstool and side tables or a coffee table can also be included.

There are no hard and fast rules about what type of seating one should select for today's country house, but you'll find that most country living rooms boast simple, sturdy, oversized sofas and deep-seated armchairs, as the emphasis in this room should be very much on comfort. Overstuffed items are in order, as are classic designs that have stood the test of time, such as an old, well-worn leather chesterfield. The idea is not to perch primly on the edge but to sink deep into the seat. Delicate, design-led furniture has no place in the country-style living room. One or two period pieces could be included, but this would be more for their decorative appeal than the fact that they are traditional country items.

below This built-in cupboard has been cleverly planned to blend in with the interior design of the room, as its sides are made of slim planks of wood painted white, while the door fronts remain plain.

right Several highly contrasting pillows increase both the comfort of the sofa and the visual interest in this predominantly white room.

Apart from seating, other furniture may also be used in the living room, especially given today's requirement for extensive storage space. Again, your selection of these items may not be true to a country cottage aesthetic, but tables, cupboards, and shelving should still be in keeping with a bygone era. Wood, be it pine or polished, always has a place in the country home, but other materials such as wicker, rattan, or, to a certain extent, wrought iron can also be used. The natural qualities of these materials make them suitable choices.

Continuing the theme of comfort, it goes without saying that chairs and sofas in particular should be piled high with pillows. Don't skimp on these—one meager pillow in the corner of the sofa will not convey the idea of comfort. What you need is a whole pile—enough to make you want to dive in and snuggle up, should the mood take you. Recently, throws have found a place in the country house. In days of old, their use in modest cottages was to cover up and protect the user from drafts, but today their purpose is more decorative. One or two slung over the back of the sofa lend a casual air to the room and offer a way to add color and texture to the interior. Wool, cotton, and chenille, all of which have wonderful tactile qualities, are popular fabrics for throws. Two or three of these fabrics used together are perfect for the country living room.

The size of the pattern rather than the pattern itself is really what should be taken into consideration when planning the interior design of a country living room. Use the larger, bolder patterns over the bigger expanses in the room, for example on the

opposite The most amazing things about this room are its abundance of beams, both in the ceiling and in the walls, and its prolific use of kilim rugs and pillows.

left It is quite easy to see that this is an original ceiling, where the beams have been left exposed and just the undersides of the floorboards on the upper story of the house have been plastered.

right A kilim rug has been used like a throw and placed over the back of this old velvet sofa. A kilim-style pillow in the corner continues the Eastern-inspired theme.

sofa or at the window. Then team smaller prints together for the accessories such as tiebacks, pillows, and tablecloths. Abundance is the key here: billowing curtains, piles of pillows, tablecloths touching the floor and perhaps overlaid with shorter cloths. Sofas and chairs may be upholstered, but nothing suits country style better than slipcovers. On a practical note they make cleaning easier, and if you're living a true country life elements of the outdoors will soon make their way into the interior of your house. Muddy paw prints and dog hairs on the sofa are just a couple of reasons for slipcovers, but they also give furniture the unstructured look typical of the country house. And if these covers include ruffles or pleats, or need ties to hold them in place, so much the better. Notice how, in the room shown opposite, the window seat has a box-pleated skirt and is piled with cushions and pillows, yet the finish, far from being overdone, looks attractive and inviting.

Don't chuck out the chintz!

Living rooms in wealthier homes have always been showcases for the display of the owners' taste and wealth—so if you want to go to town with interior decorating, then this is the room in which to do so. But leave all ideas about coordination at the door—this is not the place to create a color scheme based on all the usual principles of interior design. In fact, the more eclectic the mix, the better the

opposite This living room is a perfect example of how fabrics can be mixed and matched successfully in the country house despite featuring a wide range of patterns. Here damask, chintz, checks, and tapestry have all been cleverly combined.

left Chintz fabric epitomizes the country look. Ornate window treatments such as swags are too elaborate. Simply hanging curtains on a wooden pole is all that is required in the country house.

right A circle of glass is used to form a table top. It keeps the cloth in place and also prevents it from getting dirty. A selection of silverware and a posy of flowers make an attractive arrangement.

result, as long as you bear one thing in mind—not to incorporate late-20th-century designs into the room. Once you dispense with materials or color combinations from the latter half of the 20th century such as plastic, chrome, and monochromes, and select from the huge array of fabrics and materials that remain, then compiling a country-style living room becomes almost effortless.

Chintz is probably the fabric most people associate with the country look. Although it originally came from India, the popularity of this fabric in the West blossomed in the 18th century, and soon it was also being produced in Europe. Initially, Americans imported their chintz from England, but by the end of the 1700s it was being manufactured in the New World too. Known for its patterns depicting flowers, fruit, or birds, usually on a light-colored background, and often glazed to give it a shiny finish, this fabric was originally used mainly in mansions or manor houses. Today it has been successfully incorporated into all types of country house. Some people regard it as outdated, but there's no doubt that chintz is still key to the country-cottage feel.

Apart from chintz, materials that define the style include ginghams and other checks, tickings, and plaids such as tartan—a clothing fabric brought indoors by the Victorians, who appreciated its heavy texture and rich colors. These fabrics can all be used alongside chintz, as the marriage of floral and geometric patterns actually adds to the country interior. Tapestry, crewelwork, linen, and velvet can all be used in the living room. A mixture of textures is desirable, and teaming velvet with tapestry, cotton with crewelwork, or damask with lace and linen, produces pleasing visual and tactile results. A worn, faded finish conveys the country look better than a starchy newness so when buying fabric for curtains or pillows, why not wash it or dry-clean it a couple of times before use to take away its feeling of newness?

Window treatments

Window dressings are an important element of any room and in the country living room curtains are a must—this is not the place

Terra-cotta teamed with a hint of blue makes a powerful color scheme. Terra-cotta is a warm shade while the cool hues of blue contrast with it well. Checks and stripes, both strong designs in their own right, also work very well together.

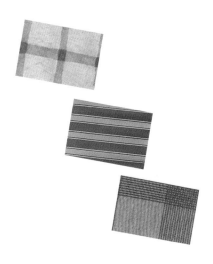

opposite *When a dense block of color could be too overpowering, colorwashing walls is a good alternative—you get the color but at a reduced strength. The leaded windows' diamond pattern works well with the checks and stripes.*

for roller or Roman shades, whose straight lines are too harsh, no matter what fabric they are made from. In fact, simple curtains are almost a must—but simple in style rather than in pattern, as anything from plaids to lively fabric designs is suitable. Unless you are dealing with large windows, elaborate draperies, cornices, or swags are much more manor house than simple country cottage. But don't skimp on the amount of fabric you use for making curtains; even when the curtains are closed, the fabric should fall in gentle folds.

When hanging curtains, you have two basic options—wooden or wrought-iron curtain poles. This is not the place for plastic curtain rods. You could perhaps use brass curtain poles, however; originally these were found in grand houses, but now brass has found its niche in more modest country homes. Use a pole in proportion to the window. A thick pole with fancy finials will work best at a large window and a simple metal pole is best at smaller windows, which are usually the type found in country cottages.

Floor treatments

For the floor it's important to go for something comfortable. Wood flooring is extremely popular in country-cottage style, but if you are pursuing true comfort then several rugs scattered on the floor are in order. In the old days, poor homes would have had rush matting or homemade rag rugs placed in front of the fire, while the floors of grander houses would have been adorned with oriental rugs and pileless woven rugs such as kilims from Turkey and dhurries from India, imported or picked up from travels abroad. Today coir, jute, and seagrass matting are popular choices for the country house, especially in the living room—despite

left *A large squashy armchair with a reading light positioned above it makes an area of comfort in a living room in which most of the other surfaces, including seating, are hard.*

below *A color scheme can be based around the building materials used in the room. Here the pink and cream tones found in the brickwork have inspired the colors chosen to decorate this room, and to make it more warm and welcoming.*

above *The pine bench is an interesting choice for the main form of seating in the living room, and has something of the church pew about it. The warm tones of the wood and bricks make the room appear inviting and attractive to the eye.*

their utilitarian appearance. Their texture and the fact that they are made from natural materials make them a good option.

Carpets would have adorned the floors of the richer homes, but wall-to-wall carpets are not really what the country feel is about. If you just can't live without carpet beneath your feet, a large square carpet in the center of the room, leaving a floorboard border around the edge, is the look you should aim for.

Favorite things

In country style, accessories, the finishing touches in any room, can come from a variety of sources, but classic items are far more likely to say country than are contemporary items fashioned from modern materials.

Items that were once intended for a practical purpose have frequently found a decorative use in the country home. Fire irons and bellows may no longer be required for lighting fires but they make an attractive display. Pictures with a country-related subject matter or items with a nostalgic feel, such as old tin advertising signs, can be used on the walls. Even a picture of a boat framed in driftwood evokes the necessary feel for country living. Likewise, family photographs framed in wood, silver, or fabric make a wonderful collection on a coffee table. Ceramics, ranging from simple flea market finds to collectible china, are a must, and novel ideas such as an urn filled with willow branches, or miniature bay trees placed on a mantelpiece work because they continue the theme of bringing the outdoors in. At the other extreme so, too, do antlers on the wall.

The most important thing in styling the living room is to surround yourself with items and furnishings that you love, and the older the better. What you want to achieve is a real living room where you're encouraged to sit on the furniture or handle the items on display, not regard them from a distance as if they were museum pieces.

right *Bringing the outdoors in is part of country style, and in here animal accessories are everywhere. Note the cowbells on the mantelpiece, the antlers in the entry hall, and the many pictures of birds, including a bird's head carved on the bellows.*

A place to relax and a place to dream. Four-poster beds, crisp cotton bedlinen, patchwork quilts, and pretty hangings are the essential elements for a peaceful and tranquil room.

BEDROOMS

Washstands and warming pans

Today's country-style bedroom still serves the same purpose as it did years ago, the difference being that now we have turned relaxation into an art form and the degree of comfort we expect from a bedroom far exceeds that required from it in the past.

A simple cottage would usually have had just one bedroom built under the rafters of the roof, and the whole family would have slept together in one bed at night. The purely functional purpose of this room, the lack of space, and the fact that for most of the year, except maybe in summer, the room would be very cold meant that no one was tempted to linger there. Even wealthier farmhouses boasted bedrooms decorated with just the bare necessities: a highly polished brass or painted iron bed with a deep horsehair or perhaps feather mattress, and a washstand with all the accoutrements necessary for washing. The tendency was to keep clothes folded up in drawers and chests, rather than to hang them in closets or wardrobes, the use of which became commonplace only in the 19th century. Bedroom furniture was often plainer in design than the items that featured in living rooms.

Rugs or floorcloths adorned the floor and the only heating in the room may have come from bringing the dying embers up

Pink is always a popular choice for the bedroom—its appeal spans generations. Hard candy pinks can be tempered with rose or blush colors, and pink always works well with cream as a contrast.

left *The bedlinen with its eyelet trim is simple and pretty, while the dust ruffle looks good being more heavily patterned.*

above Pattern is introduced into this country bedroom via the design of the wallpaper, while the curtains and bedlinen are quite plain. The fresh, delicate-looking cotton bedding shows off the striking bedsteads to their best advantage.

from the main fire to use in the smaller fireplace, if the bedroom had one at all. However, a warming pan full of hot coals was often used to warm the bed before people retired at night.

At the other extreme, grand country houses had a whole different attitude to bedrooms. Much thought was given to their decoration and they featured beautiful curtains, pillows, and bedlinen. A somewhat larger fireplace would be found in the bedroom of an upscale country house, whose owners could afford to burn a fire here before bedtime and didn't have to rely on embers to warm the room. The size of the rooms and wealth of the family meant these bedrooms could have four-poster beds. Their use today conveys luxury and romanticism but in the past four-posters were appreciated far more for their practical aspect, as the heavy bed hangings were closed to keep drafts out at night.

Once again, today's country-style bedrooms have drawn on influences from the past, combining the ideas from wealthy homes with the plain and simple appeal of cottage decor to make a room that offers the most appealing aspects of both.

Beds and bedlinen

To create a country bedroom you should begin with a bed that looks inviting. This can be achieved in several ways. If you prefer more opulent styles, then, a four-poster bed is a must, space permitting. Whether you choose to use hangings on it is a personal decision, as, thanks to central heating, you are unlikely to

Bringing a deeper, earthy shade of pink into the color scheme is a good idea if you want a color that will enhance any wood that is found within the bedroom.

left *The zigzag pattern and use of quite bright pinks as well as pastel shades makes this bedcover appear modern in its design. However, it certainly looks at home in this grand bedroom.*

right *The use of cornices is more country manor than country cottage, and they work best at large windows such as this. The scalloped edge gives the cornice a softer finish than a straight edge would.*

below *This bedroom has an opulent look thanks to the dark wood furniture, bold cornice, and variety of rich fabrics throughout the room. Many of the furnishings have quite different heritages but work well together here because the pink color scheme unifies them.*

need them for purely practical reasons. Hangings do present a wonderful opportunity to create a bed with romantic appeal. Simple white curtains can look crisp and fresh, while patterned heavier fabrics will give the room a more opulent air. An alternative idea is to make hangings from muslin. This cloth, long popular in country communities, has been given a new lease on life recently as a favorite fabric for fashionable homes. Swags of muslin suspended above a bed can create an instant curtain, taking its inspiration from the mosquito net.

Even if your budget doesn't stretch to a four-poster bed, simple beds made from pine, iron, or brass are all perfectly acceptable and each in its own way suits the country theme. Pine was used for furniture in rooms of lesser importance and was usually found in the homes of most poor people. Today pine furniture has been adopted as the wood of choice for country-style interiors. Many country-style bedrooms boast not just a pine bed, but chests of drawers and wardrobes too. Failing that, a modern bed can be made to look the part provided it is given appropriate bedlinen and looks comfortable and inviting.

Choose your bedlinen carefully. The country bedroom isn't the place for modern printed duvet covers in garish designs, even if they are floral. Old-fashioned bedlinen may be hard work, as making a bed with sheets and blankets is far harder than simply shaking out a duvet, but if you really want your bedroom to be authentic then this is what you should aim for. In the past many cottagers grew their own flax. Flax was spun into linen and used to make bedlinen. Now linen is relatively expensive, with linen sheets considered a luxury, and crisp cotton sheets have become the mainstay of the country bedroom. The addition of lace or embroidery lends a softer, more homemade look to the sheets and you should aim to choose this type of bedding, or consider adding lace trim or simple embroidery yourself. Make sure you opt for piles of pillows on the bed, as an abundance of these will convey the opulent look you're after. Skimping in this area will detract from the overall style of the room.

The bedroom should also appeal to your sense of smell. Finishing touches should include fresh flowers, potpourri, and lavender bags. The

left *The intricate quilting makes this fantastic bedspread very appealing. Cleverly, it echoes the barley-sugar twist pedestal of the table used as a nightstand, which itself is stunning in its simplicity.*

country home was often a fragrant one—not just because of the food cooking on the range, but because of the ease with which it was possible to bring the outdoors in.

The patchwork quilt

If there's one item that has become essential to the country bedroom it must be the patchwork quilt. When you think how many hours of hard labor went into making these by hand—sometimes by groups of women in a community, or by a family getting together to work on just one item—then it seems amazing that beautiful vintage patchwork quilts are still available today at reasonable prices. You could quite easily buy a new quilt and achieve the country look in an instant, but if you wish to incorporate some craft, nostalgia, and history into your bedroom, then buying a more costly secondhand patchwork quilt or even making your own will give you the results that no mass-produced item can ever offer. The beauty of original patchwork quilts is that they were made from scraps of material from old, worn clothes or curtains, but also may have included fabric from a wedding dress, christening gown, child's clothing, or other such treasured items of sentimental value.

There are no strict rules about how to decorate the actual bedroom itself. Remember that the most common time for you to see this room in all its glory is in the morning, so the look you'll

opposite Sometimes all it takes is just one or two interesting items to give a room appeal. Here the patchwork quilt and unusual bedstead do just that, and this otherwise plain bedroom is saved from verging on the ordinary.

left Patchwork quilts are actually made up in two stages. First the design is made up from "patches" of fabric being "pieced" together. Then when it is finished, all the layers are quilted together. The stitches form a decorative pattern themselves.

right A wonderful bedstead such as this is a feature in its own right. However, a few well-chosen small accessories always bring an old-fashioned feeling to a country room.

want to go for is one that is fresh, clean, and pretty—one that will reflect the light and the sun coming into the room. Dark colors or heavy patterns aren't ideal as they'll absorb too much light. Creams, pinks, and yellows, or any pastel shades are well suited to the bedroom. Wallpapers with delicate designs such as sprigs of flowers work well in here, and if you're decorating an irregular-shaped room such as an attic bedroom you may even want to take the paper up onto the ceiling too. This doesn't mean that some carefully chosen bright colors or busy patterns can't be used—they can work well in a country bedroom, especially if the room is large enough for the print to be displayed to its best advantage. After all, country manor houses and stately homes were known for their exquisite bedrooms with gorgeous wall coverings and draperies at the window.

Bedroom furniture

Chairs are an important item of furniture in country-style bedrooms—anything from a simple wooden seat to a wicker chair or even a soft upholstered armchair. Again, the choice depends on the space available. Just be sure to make them appear inviting through the addition of a cushion or seat pad. Other seating ideas include window seats, an ottoman, or a blanket box or hope chest

left The only bright colors found in this lovely bedroom come from this delightful vase of fresh flowers. Change the flowers, and you change the color scheme!

right Wood and white make up the color scheme in here, and very successful it is too. The best way to show the bed off is to make sure nothing competes with it, and by choosing simple white furnishings nothing does.

above Using a mini-print wallpaper and the same pattern for the curtain fabric unifies the color scheme and makes the most of the space in a small bedroom, where the use of large patterns or bold designs can be overpowering.

with a soft seat pad placed on its lid, usually positioned at the end of the bed. For something more dramatic choose a chaise-longue. They may not have been found in the traditional country house, but having become popular in the early 1800s, they are now considered rather decadent, as the idea of relaxing during the daytime isn't in vogue. Washstands make a delightful addition. Though no longer required for their original purpose, they serve as a charming display area and can look extremely attractive with ceramics, flowers, or photographs arranged on the top. A small writing desk may well have been found, particularly in guest bedrooms of grand country houses, and if there's room for one in yours it's also a lovely item to stand in front of the window—it may even inspire you to write occasionally.

Wickerwork was popular in Victorian times, and this type of furniture is particularly suited to the bedroom, as the open-weave designs of rattan, cane, and wicker give it a softer, lighter appearance than wooden furniture. The result is that furniture made from these materials works well in any size of bedroom, where the need for heavy, robust items isn't as important as in other rooms of the house. These natural materials also add to the country image, as they are reminiscent of a time when craftsmen would have made items from these materials for use in their own and other local homes.

Burnt orange, beige, and wheat make for a demure color scheme. When you're decorating small rooms, neutrals and naturals are always a good choice, as paler colors make the room seem larger.

left *These curtains are one of the simplest styles you can find, as the tops are devoid of any fussy details. Hung on a wooden curtain pole, they are perfect for a country-style bedroom.*

right *White china with simple floral motifs makes an attractive display on an old washstand situated in a corner of this little bedroom.*

Bedroom lighting

Years ago candles, and later kerosene or oil lamps, would have been the only form of lighting in bedrooms or often the whole house, and today these can be included, though their presence often lends a more romantic than practical element to the design scheme. Central overhead lighting is often too harsh, particularly at night, and not in keeping with true country style. Electricity started to be used for lighting in the early 1900s, but it would have been much later before most country cottages enjoyed its convenience. Lamps are more suitable for bedroom lighting. Bases made from wood, brass, or ceramics coupled with classic coolie shades made from fabrics such as chintz, silk, burlap, or even handmade paper look best. Avoid lamps in materials and

left Pretty mini-print fabrics have been used to decorate this bedroom. Although the patterns differ between the curtains, tablecloth, and quilt, they work well together because the colors and dimensions unify them.

above *Crisp white bedlinen makes this bed look inviting, and it complements the dark wood very well. The small but attractive window doesn't require curtains as it makes quite a feature left plain. The tiny child's chair also adds interest to this bedroom.*

left *The checked curtains are partially tucked away behind the high headboard of this bed. Originally closed to keep the cold out at night, they are used for decorative purposes now that most country houses are heated.*

colors that will look too modern—such as primary colors, plastics, chrome, and modern metals like aluminum.

A child's bedroom

In times gone by, if children were lucky enough to have their own bedroom, then it would have been quite a functional room, with a bed, a nightstand, a chest of drawers, perhaps a small chair, and little else. Today, however, creating a country-style bedroom for children is a pure delight. It's a chance to bring all the sweetest elements of country style together—pastel colors on the wall, delicate floral motifs or tiny checks and stripes for fabrics and wall coverings, natural flooring that'll stand up to the wear and tear only children are capable of giving, and simple wooden furniture, perhaps painted or decorated with stencils or folk-art inspired motifs. Original nursery furniture is quite hard to come by but worth searching for. A straw basket, bassinet, or tiny nursery chairs make charming additions to these rooms— even when the occupants have long since outgrown them!

left Teddy bears always have a place in a child's bedroom. Those made of patchwork, or a little battered and worn, look particularly at home in the country house.

right Stone walls painted lavender and teamed with balloon-patterned wallpaper in mint green make a stunning combination for a child's bedroom. White bedlinen is a must for children's rooms too.

There's a lot of decorating fun to be had in
here, as the source of ideas for this room need
never run dry. From Victorian style to seaside
simplicity you'll find these country bathrooms
offer plenty of novel ideas.

BATHROOMS

above Paneled walls and an attractive chair rail teamed with a taupe seashell-patterned wallpaper—a design reflected in the choice of towels—make for a stylish and practical bathroom with a seaside theme.

Bathing Victorian-style

A place to wash, clean, maybe even lie back and dream. As a personal retreat from a busy, tough, and often dirty outdoor life, the country-style bathroom provides a much-needed element of escapism.

The bathroom is actually a room that wouldn't have existed at all in many country homes until the 20th century, so the style in which we decorate it has evolved from Victorian and turn-of-the-century ideas, as this was the time when bathrooms started to become more commonplace in the home. It is possible that some of the very richest country homes had indoor bathrooms before then. The decor, however, would have been inspired by styles of the time. Therefore it could be said that the country bathroom is in some ways a contradiction in terms, as the look we refer to as "country bathroom" was rarely found in country homes at all until relatively recently.

It was only during the 20th century that the bathroom became a familiar indoor feature. Until then, whether you were rich or poor your toilet remained outside in the "outhouse," which might be right at the far side of the yard. To save a trip down the garden path at night most people kept a chamber pot under the bed. Washing was done indoors using a pitcher and bowl at a washstand. Baths were not taken with the regularity they are today—the old joke "if you're taking a bath it must be your birthday" wasn't far from the truth. And when baths were taken, the whole bathing process was usually carried out in a portable hip bath indoors, in front of a burning fire, upstairs in the bedroom for the rich, and in the kitchen, wash-house, or scullery for the poor.

This method of bathing was incredibly time-consuming. The water that was needed to fill the bath had to be heated first over the kitchen fire, or in later days over the wood or coal stove or the range. The bath would then have to be filled, and of course emptied, by hand—an arduous task, but only the rich could afford the luxury of maids or servants to do this job for them.

above *An attractive shelf is made by placing a simple plank of wood on two ornate wrought-iron shelf supports.*

below *A wrought-iron chair like this with a rattan seat is more commonly found outdoors or in a sunroom, but it is also perfectly at home in the bathroom.*

Of course, most old country homes weren't designed or built with bathrooms in mind, so when in Victorian times with the advent of indoor plumbing and sewerage systems the concept of the bathroom was introduced, it had to be sited in an unused bedroom or a dressing room. The Victorians would decorate it just like any other room in the house. Not surprisingly, wallpaper and floor coverings did not fare too well in damp and steamy conditions. The actual toiletries were hidden away in a wooden encasement that had the appearance of an ordinary piece of furniture, such was the prudery of the Victorians. Country-style bathrooms are now decorated as thoughtfully as any other room in the house, but without the peculiarity of hiding all essential items, and with more of an eye to practical concerns.

Since bathrooms were originally sited in an existing room of the house, they were often larger than the tiny rooms we are used to today. These rooms would boast a variety of features, such as a fireplace or window overlooking a good view, again in complete contrast to the modern purpose-built little rooms, which may not contain a window at all. Because many country bathrooms are today still sited in what would once have been a bedroom, or perhaps in the converted loft space of a barn or stable, architectural elements such as sloping ceilings and exposed beams may well remain as features.

Modern, streamlined, built-in cabinets are not for the country-style bathroom. Just as with the country kitchen, freestanding storage, as much as is possible, is far more in keeping with country style.

left *The pelmet over the shelves displaying seashells is itself decorated with shells, a motif that is echoed in the attractive stencil around the mirror.*

right *This tiny bathroom looks lovely painted pink. The woven-fiber chair makes a delightful addition, contrasting well and adding some comfort.*

above *A cream color scheme and traditional fixtures create a country-style bathroom. Color is added via the accessories and comfort comes from the grand Windsor chair.*

The cast-iron bath

The ideal type of bath to have in your country bathroom is a Victorian rolltop, cast-iron bath. Originally these were encased in wooden frames. Should you choose to do this, a rich mahogany bath panel is perfect for conveying the look of Victorian splendor. However, the practice of raising the bath on ornamental ball-and-claw feet has become extremely popular again today. The exposed underside of the bath can then be decorated to suit the color scheme of the room; or as a decorative alternative a paint-effect finish such as rag rolling, or a stencil design, perhaps incorporating a motif echoed elsewhere in the room, can look fantastic.

Space permitting, the best way to position a rolltop, cast-iron bath is to show it off in all its glory in the middle of the bathroom or beneath a window where bathers can enjoy the scenery as they wash. As a result of the growing fashion for rolltop baths, many reproduction models are now available, so it is no longer necessary to scour architectural salvage yards to find one. Failing this, an ordinary cast-iron or enamel bath can be installed to evoke the feeling of a bygone age.

Adapting the modern bath

If your bathroom does feature a modern acrylic bath then all is not lost. Generally speaking, modern colored acrylic suites are not really appropriate for country-style bathrooms, but if you have inherited acrylic fixtures, disguise is the best remedy. Simply paneling the bath, swapping the plastic toilet seat for one made of

left *Privacy is essential in the bathroom but it's a pity to replace pretty windows with patterned glass. A shade such as this with a lively floral design is a good alternative.*

right *A simple skirt made from cotton secured around the sink hides all the pipework beneath and makes a pretty addition to the bathroom.*

below Dark wood looks very stylish and quite masculine in the bathroom, but decorative details such as the cherub designs in the corner and plenty of plants prevent the room from looking too severe.

pine, and attaching a fabric skirt around the sink to hide the pedestal on which it rests can make all the difference. By clever color scheming, avocado green or canary yellow fixtures can actually be made to work in a country bathroom; after all, these are in essence country colors, even though fixtures such as these wouldn't originally have been found in country houses. If you're blessed with bathroom fixtures in a stronger shade such as purple, it might be better to give them an upscale Victoriana-inspired makeover with plenty of dark wood paneling, and a deep, rich color scheme—more country manor than country house.

Bathroom fixtures

It was only at the turn of the 20th century that the ceramic sink mounted on brackets became commonplace in the bathroom. Until then washing was done using water held in a pitcher and bowl at a washstand in the bedroom. The washstand was usually made of wood and sometimes had a marble top. To convey a country feel it is perfectly possible to have a modern working sink plumbed into into an old washstand, which combines the convenience of the new with the appearance of the old.

Generally speaking, the fixtures you should go for are those based on Victorian or turn-of-the-century styles. Avoid anything too grand—modest designs are more in keeping with the country house. A high-level tank above the toilet may be authentic, but in a country cottage you might not be able to fit one in because of the low ceilings in these buildings. Should it be possible, however, it may still appear inappropriate in a room that is otherwise down-to-earth in its design.

Simple colors, natural materials

As the bathroom is a place to relax and cleanse yourself, a simple color scheme is often the preferred choice. White or cream is a popular choice, giving a fresh feel, and setting off all other colors, as well as the colors of wood—from the yellow hues of pine through to the dark tones of mahogany. Colors that also look good in the

below *Reflected in the mirror you can see a dresser that boasts a marble top, and dark green tiles which help inject a bit of color into the bathroom.*

bathroom are blues and greens, because of their obvious associations with water, and soft pastel shades such as pink, lilac, or lemon. These can look very pretty and are fun to play with in small cottage bathrooms, as their appearance makes a little room look quite appealing.

There is no place more suited to pine paneling than the bathroom. Use it around the bath, to box in pipework, plumbing, or the toilet tank, and on the walls (either just on the lower half up to chair-rail height, or all the way up to the ceiling). Once it has been given a coat of varnish to make it waterproof, tongue-and-groove paneling is the perfect choice for the country bathroom interior. Wood looks fresh, clean, and natural and is preferable to tiles, which seem rather out of place in the country bathroom. You might get away with judiciously using a few tiles, particularly hand-painted rustic designs, for a backsplash behind the sink, but avoid tiling the whole room—the results would be far too modern and clinical. If yours is a busy family bathroom, a few rows of tiles around the bath may be in order, but otherwise they are best avoided when creating a country-style feel.

The beauty of pine paneling is that if an all-wood finish isn't to your taste, the paneling can be colorwashed to allow the grain of the wood to show through. Other possibilities include pickling it to give it a pale white finish, staining it with wood stain in any of a variety of surprisingly sophisticated shades, or simply painting it any color you choose.

Most of the bathrooms shown here are striking in their simplicity. White walls are combined with mahogany wood and

opposite The window dressings, opulent gold-framed mirror, and large bouquet of flowers combine to give this bathroom a very stylish, feminine appearance.

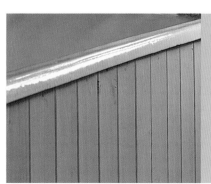

left *Pine tongue-and-groove paneling is perfect for boxing in the bath. It can be left plain, or stained, varnished, or painted in a variety of ways to suit your color scheme.*

right *Lengths of fabrics, layered at the window to form a loosely draped swag, are simply wound around a metal pole.*

below This all-white bathroom looks clean and refreshing and shows off the original beams to their best advantage. The look is prevented from appearing too clinical by the addition of plenty of accessories.

mirror panels, a room is simply painted candy pink, or white paneling is teamed with a quaint miniature-print wallpaper.

Furniture and accessories

Marine themes are always at home in the country bathroom. Obvious ways in which a seaside style can be introduced are with a blue-and-white color scheme, or via a display of seashells, pebbles, or other beach paraphernalia. Painting paneling white also imparts a marine feel, and because the seashore is part of nature, it is a theme that works well in a country-style bathroom. To continue the theme, accessories such as mirrors or bath racks made from driftwood, or fabrics and wallpapers with motifs of shells, fish, or nautical symbols could be chosen.

Window treatments can vary from having nothing at all at the windows, to simple floral cotton curtains teamed with a valance in a contrasting floral fabric, or ornate layers of sheer fabrics such as lightweight muslin or voile, arranged to make a soft, romantic swagged effect.

Additional furniture and accessories are important in the country-style bathroom because what you are trying to create is a safe haven and a place for relaxation. So, unless space is really at a

left and below *A little cupboard filled with perfumes and makeup makes a nice display, and bowls and arrangements of shells are all interesting. Even the pot of petunias is coordinated with the color scheme.*

premium, the room can benefit from having an easy chair in the corner—perhaps an old wicker chair painted white. If space is limited, a little wrought-iron chair or a stool will work well. A seat provides somewhere to relax while young children bathe, or at the very least a place to pile clothes instead of on the floor. Tables or shelves can be used to show off collections as well as provide storage for bathroom essentials such as mirrors, brushes, and toiletries. Bath racks, commonly used in Victorian times, are a welcome addition to the country bathroom, particularly if they are made of wood. A slatted pine duckboard on the floor makes a suitable alternative to a bathmat, although a small rag rug is an authentic addition. Wooden clotheshorses were used in Victorian bathrooms, and a contemporary pine version, or a quilt rack, is perfect placed in front of the window to hold towels. Modern-day necessities such as shower curtains are best made from cotton fabric and lined with plastic to make them waterproof, as the plastic versions have no place in a country-style setting. An alternative decorative idea is to use a Victorian screen, which would have been used to change behind in the bedroom, as a screen for bathing behind.

Don't forget to inject a bit of life and nature into the bathroom with well-chosen flowers and plants. Many plants enjoy the humid atmosphere of the bathroom, and a simple bunch of flowers can make all the difference. You'll notice how all the bathrooms featured here contain either plants or flowers, which is very much part of their appeal.

opposite Even the beams have been painted white in this all-white bathroom. A few oriental accessories, dotted here and there, make the room more interesting.

left This tiny window needs no curtains as it looks out over rooftops. A pot plant is all that's required by way of decoration.

right Old-fashioned faucets suit the sink in this bathroom, and the tiny Shaker-inspired peg rail on the wall is the perfect place for hand towels.

PICTURE CREDITS

The author and publishers are grateful to Elizabeth Whiting Associates and to the following photographers for their kind permission to reproduce the photographs on the following pages: 2, 11, 13, 30, 32–3, 36–8, 46, 58–9, 85–7, 90–3 Lu Jeffrey; 6, 14–15, 29, 77, 84 Spike Powell; 8, 63, 68, 72–3, 81 Di Lewis; 9 16–17, 22, 40–1, 64–5 Michael Dunne; 18, 50–51 Mark Luscombe-Whyte; 20–21, 31, 34–5, 82–3, 88–9 Dennis Stone; 24–5 Tim Beddow; 27, 31, 48–9 Nick Carter; 42–3, 86 Andreas v. Einsiedel; 45, 54–6, 66–7 Brian Harrison; 52–3, 61, 78–9 Simon Upton; 70–1 EWA; 74–5 Huntley Hedworth; 76 Nadia MacKenzie; 94–5 Bruce Hemmings.